pixelgarten

La collection design&designer est éditée par
PYRAMYD NTCV
15, rue de Turbigo
75002 Paris, France

Tél. : 33 (0)1 40 26 00 99
Fax : 33 (0)1 40 26 00 79
www.pyramyd-editions.com

Direction éditoriale : Michel Chanaud, Céline Remechido
Traduction : Sasha Barral
Correction : Marie-Christine Montesquat (FR), Sara Brady (UK)
Conception graphique du livre : Sarah Bruey
Conception graphique de la couverture : Pyramyd NTCV
Conception graphique de la collection : Super Cinq
Pictogrammes de la collection : Thibault Geffroy

ISBN : 978-2-35017-233-0
ISSN : 1636-8150
Dépôt légal : avril 2011

Imprimé en Italie par Lego

pixelgarten

préfacé par vanina pinter

Avec Pixelgarten, le design graphique s'aventure sur la scène des arts vivants. À ce préjugé souvent énoncé par les commanditaires : « Aujourd'hui avec un ordinateur, il faut une heure pour réaliser une image », Pixelgarten réagit avec sourire. Il leur propose de remonter et de prendre le temps. Le duo allemand s'installe dans une pièce, déroule un câble électrique pour écrire une phrase, invente un paysage dans un coin de studio, uniquement avec des morceaux de papiers, trois bouts de Scotch, quelques objets dépareillés. Au fil de leur production artistique, le contenu de la boîte à outils du graphiste est répertoriée, mais au lieu d'apparaître à l'écran de l'ordinateur, leur œuvre se répand dans l'espace, la peinture des bombes de couleurs dégouline, les icônes des dossiers numériques se matérialisent… Impossible avec Pixelgarten de réduire le design graphique à une technique. Ils sont prêts à se pasticher en donnant un corps humain à la technologie 3D – un carton sur la tête pour le prouver. Évidemment, on sent s'exprimer une pointe d'ironie sur un métier qui ne serait qu'appliqué et sur un monde qui perdrait à sombrer dans le virtuel. Mais l'injonction est ailleurs. Au lieu de sombrer dans l'engrenage actuel et de tout concevoir vite, Pixelgarten incite à inventer, constamment, le plus simplement possible, avec poésie, en procurant du plaisir au regardeur.

With Pixelgarten, graphic design ventures into the world of performing arts. The phrase we often hear from clients, "It only takes an hour to make an image with a computer nowadays," just makes the Pixelgarten designers smile. They propose taking a step back and slowing things down. The German pair sets themselves up in a room and writes sentences in unrolled electricity cable or creates a landscape in a studio corner with just a few scraps of paper, three bits of Sellotape and a few mismatched objects. They use just about every graphic design tool available in their work, but rather than displaying their work on a computer screen, they spread it out into real space with dripping spray cans and folder icons in material form.

It's impossible to narrow down Pixelgarten's graphic design to just one technique. They use their own bodies to give 3-D technology human form – and there's the box over the head to prove it. There's clearly a touch of irony here (about a profession that is considered to be an "applied" art and a world that has drifted into virtual space). But the intention is different. Instead of getting sucked into a downward spiral of doing everything faster, Pixelgarten invites us to be creative – constantly, poetically and as simply as possible, for the viewer's pleasure.

UN ART DE SALTIMBANQUE

En 2003, le graphiste autrichien installé à New York, Stefan Sagmeister, élabore pour un concours organisé par Adobe, une affiche pour le moins surprenante. Au lieu de vanter les prouesses techniques, il clame la suprématie de l'ingéniosité individuelle. Avec son assistant, ils installent sur le sol 2 500 gobelets blancs, remplis ou non de café, noir ou au lait, et ces derniers prennent la forme d'une coupe (il s'agit d'annoncer un concours de création primé : Adobe Design Achievement Awards). Un échafaudage de plusieurs mètres de hauteur est installé pour prendre une photographie en plongée et mémoriser cet énorme trophée de plastique et de caféine. Un cliché, une typographie en gobelets, une couronne de laurier et l'affiche fait le tour du monde. La démesure du travail fascine. Le procédé défie les prouesses de l'ordinateur. Dans une verve différente, les dispositifs à « trois francs six sous » – toujours complexes dans leur processus – du réalisateur de clips musicaux Michel Gondry sont de formidables machines à rêves.

Très vite, une nouvelle génération apparaît. Ils doutent des effets uniformes des logiciels de PAO pour revenir à la matière et renouveler le genre de l'illustration. Tout en se servant du numérique à bon escient, ils interrogent nos comportements, mettent en exergue le processus de travail. Cependant, il

AN ACROBATIC ART FORM

In 2003, Stefan Sagmeister, an Austrian designer living in New York, devised a rather unusual poster for a competition organised by Adobe. Rather than vaunting his technical skills, he demonstrated his personal ingenuity. With help from his assistant, he placed 2,500 coffee cups (black, white and milk only) on the floor in the shape of a trophy as an advertisement for a design competition, the Adobe Design Achievement Awards. He set up scaffolding several metres high and took a high-angle shot to record his gigantic paper-cup-and-caffeine trophy. The photograph, with coffee-cup typography and a laurel crown, travelled all around the world. The excessiveness of the work fascinated people. The process challenged the capabilities of the computer. In a different vein, the music video director Michel Gondry's "garage band" aesthetic devices (always with complex design processes) are their own fantastic dream machines.

A new generation is appearing fast. It questions the uniform effects of DTP software and advocates a return to physical materials and a revival of the illustrative genre. While continuing to use computer tools wisely, they question our behaviour and place the emphasis on the work process. However, this isn't just a case of simply

ne s'agit pas de mettre dos à dos numérique et méthodes/outils traditionnels : au contraire, les deux ont besoin de se côtoyer, de se mêler pour créer un art aussi personnel que contemporain. « Les objets réalisés à la main sont magnifiques, car ils sont imparfaits, ils parlent de la personne qui les a créés. »

Ce fut presque un vent de panique, une résurgence dans le domaine graphique, que Pixelgarten honora et marqua en faisant la couverture du recueil *Tactile*, édité par DGV, ainsi qu'en participant aux choix des graphistes sélectionnés dans cet ouvrage.

L'esprit facétieux, dans leur œuvre, est presque tangible. Ils s'amusent, se mettent en scène en se parodiant. Au départ, ils prirent le nom de « pixelgarten » avec l'intention de créer un site web interactif qui serait un espace d'échanges et de constructions. Chacun serait à même d'y planter un travail et de le faire vivre. Le pixel n'était pas pris comme un genre formel, mais comme une unité universelle de communication. Le jardin ne vit jamais le jour, les deux graphistes furent de suite embarqués dans la production. De l'intention, ils ne conservèrent que le nom.

Adrian Niessler et Catrin Altenbrandt se sont rencontrés lors de leurs études à l'université d'art et de design (Hochschule für Gestaltung) d'Offenbach. L'enseignement y est pensé dans la lignée du

using computer tools and traditional methods and tools back to back, but of mixing them and merging them into a personal and contemporary art form. For this: "Handmade objects are fantastic because they are so imperfect, they tell us something about the person who made them."

What was almost a wave of panic and resurgence in graphic art was recorded and honoured by Pixelgarten on the cover of the *Tactile* collection, published by DGV, a collection of work in which they are featured with other, selected graphic designers. Their mischievous style is almost tangible in their works. They play, put on disguises and make fun of themselves. Originally, the name Pixelgarten was intended for an interactive website for exchange and construction. People were supposed to plant something on the site and then look after it. The pixel wasn't considered in a formal sense, but as a unit of universal communication. However, the garden never became a reality. The two designers immediately swept into production. In the end, they just kept the name.

Adrian Niessler and Catrin Altenbrandt met while studying at the Offenbach Academy of Art and Design. The school's teaching method is based on Bauhaus ideas and promotes interdisciplinarity and close relationships

Bauhaus, avec cet idéal d'interdisciplinarité et de proximité des sections. « Du fait qu'il était possible de mélanger art, installation, photographie et design graphique, cela nous a permis de produire des formes et des illustrations dans l'espace réel. Avec du recul, c'était un lieu idéal pour étudier, nous y avions la liberté nécessaire pour développer notre propre positionnement. » Ils sont des artisans avant tout. Ils jouent constamment à nous promener de la 3D à la 2D. Comme l'écran et ses logiciels sont pour eux des outils trop limités, ils trouvent dans la réalité, la matière, le plaisir de varier les connexions et les outils, d'aviver constamment notre curiosité. Pixelgarten se distingue par le jeu qu'il propose et par lequel il provoque toujours le lecteur. Il l'invite à se plonger dans leurs paysages réels et fictifs. Dans *Hoehenluft*, illustrant un article sur les mythes de l'Everest, le duo nous propulse dans les montagnes enneigées. À travers différentes saynètes, le vertige s'installe. Nous sommes face à de minuscules personnages perdus dans cette immensité blanche. Mais l'immensité se réduit quand on s'aperçoit qu'elle est formée par un corps humain drapé (celui de Catrin). Rajoutant du dessin à leur installation, ils prolongent la magie du lieu, tout en y révélant la face cachée : la réalité d'un tourisme à la Disney.

between the sections. "The fact that it was possible to mix art, installation, photography and graphic design allowed us to produce forms and illustrations in real space. In hindsight, it was the perfect place to study – we had the freedom we needed to develop our own approach." First and foremost Pixelgarten's designers are craftsmen who constantly push our vision between 3-D and 2-D spaces. Limited by the screen and its software, they take pleasure in the variety of connections and tools that can be found in reality and material forms, which continually arouse our curiosity. Pixelgarten stands out for its clever design, which always provokes the viewer. They invite us to plunge into real and fictional landscapes. For *Hoehenluft*, a set of illustrations for an article about legendary Mount Everest expeditions, the duo propels us into the snow-capped mountains. As you stare at the small scenes you get a dizzying feeling of height. In the immense white landscape there are miniscule people lost in the snow. But the feeling of immensity subsides when you realise that the mountains are formed by a human body draped with a sheet (Catrin's). By adding drawing to their installation, they manage to enhance the scene's magic while revealing its hidden side – a kind of "Disneyland-esque" reality. When I look at their work, I often reference the performing arts and especially the circus. For good reason, just

J'ai souvent invoqué, au vu de leurs productions, l'art du spectacle vivant, et notamment le cirque. Et pour cause, remarquez la parade. Telles les pitreries de ce moustique (illustration pour le magazine *Neon*) qui baigne dans son papier de sang. Ailleurs, un livre s'est déguisé en moustachu sérieux. Ils donnent au cinquantième numéro du magazine allemand *Form* un caractère festif et burlesque. Les couleurs sont vives. Tout se dérègle, les objets tombent, les projections bariolées éclaboussent. Le studio manie avec une dextérité certaine l'art de la dissimulation et du maquillage. Catrin et Adrian oscillent souvent, avec malice, entre montrer ce qui se trouve derrière les ficelles ou le cacher pour laisser l'imagination vagabonder. La série *A Look Back at 2008*, réalisée pour *Neon*, transpose cette grosse machinerie qu'est la communication dans l'univers des gants blancs du magicien. Dernièrement, des objets entrent en lévitation pour devenir des natures mortes illustrant les mois d'un calendrier 2011.

L'erreur est souvent invoquée pour provoquer le sourire et questionner (comme au cirque). Mais le numéro est toujours parfaitement orchestré : ce sont des passionnés, ils ont répété, contrôlé, surveillé le moindre morceau de papier. Le temps est planifié, les erreurs réajustées. L'ordinateur supervise l'ensemble. L'improvisation est impossible, car la moindre erreur oblige à reconstruire l'installation.

take a look at some examples: the dumbass mosquito (illustration for *Neon* magazine) bathing in its own paper blood, a book wearing a serious-looking moustache, and the 50th edition of the German magazine *Form* with its festive, comical style. The colours are bright. Everything is off balance, objects fall over and rainbow-coloured projections spatter everywhere. The studio is particularly skilful with makeup and their own particular brand of deception. Catrin and Adrian swing between the delight of revealing their trade secrets and that of hiding them to let our imaginations run wild. A series they made for *Neon* magazine, "A Look Back at 2008," takes the great machine of mass communication and transposes it into the world of a white-gloved magician. More recently, objects have started to levitate and become still life to illustrate months in a 2011 calendar. Often they use "error" to make us smile and ask questions (like the circus). But the act is always perfectly orchestrated: these enthusiasts practise, control and monitor the tiniest shred of paper. Their timing is perfect, the errors are just so. The computer oversees the whole. Improvisation is impossible, because one tiny mistake means building the installation from scratch. Some images require a week of preparation (e.g., "Super Mario Fashion" for *Neon* magazine). In their more ephemeral acts they make lettering out of cardboard and paper –

Certaines de leurs images nécessitent une semaine de préparatifs (par exemple, *Super Mario Fashion* pour le magazine *Neon*). Pour leur numéro éphémère, ils bricolent des typos en carton, en papier, souvent sommaires, massives et pop. Elles sont des éléments du décor, dans lequel prennent part les personnages, car leurs images sont réellement animées. Le design graphique touche alors à l'art de la performance, la performance sculpturale qu'on pourrait rattacher à certaines tendances de l'art contemporain (Erwin Wurm et ses *One Minutes Sculptures* initiées depuis 1996). Avec les natures mortes, Pixelgarten transforme le corps en sculpture. Tout devient matière. Entre art vivant et bande dessinée, la photographie a le dernier mot. Elle est le média essentiel et décisif.

Pixelgarten ne peut se réduire au seul répertoire « illustration 3D faite main ». Une grande partie de leur travail est numérique et concerne la mise en page (affiches, catalogues d'exposition). Ils prennent régulièrement en charge la direction artistique de livres, avec beaucoup de plaisir. Penser la matérialité du livre est primordial. En fonction du papier choisi, le livre peut changer totalement d'aspect. Dans ce contexte, l'un de leur premier réflexe est de choisir la typographie du projet, car elle déterminera l'intention de l'objet. Pour le design du livre sur la ville de Francfort, ils ont contourné

often basic and massive in a Pop style. These will become elements of the decor for their characters to move in (because their images really are animated). Graphic design overlaps with the performing arts and sculptural performance, which we can link with particular trends in contemporary art (Erwin Wurm and his *One Minutes Sculptures*, since 1996). In their still lifes, Pixelgarten transforms the body into sculpture. Everything becomes material; mixing the performing arts with the comic strip, but photography has the final word. It is the essential and conclusive medium.

We cannot pigeonhole Pixelgarten in the "handmade 3-D illustration" category. A large part of their work is digital and is related to layout (posters, exhibition catalogues). They regularly work as art directors on book projects and they really enjoy it. Remembering the book's material qualities is the key. A book can change completely depending on what type of paper you choose. When designing a book their first move is to choose the project's typography because this will determine the object's intention. To design a book about the city of Frankfurt, they overcame a strict institutional style by interspersing different types of illustrations amongst the

la froideur institutionnelle en rythmant la documentation à travers différents genres d'illustrations. Le studio allemand conçoit tout travail comme une zone d'expérimentations avec pour ligne de conduite d'exciter sans cesse sa réflexion. À cette fin, il préconise la variété des projets et recommande d'avoir des commanditaires qui aient l'envie et le courage d'un propos individualisé. Depuis cette année, ils interviennent en tant que professeurs invités à l'université d'art et de design d'Offenbach. Ils perpétuent ce précepte des avant-gardes : « le croisement des différentes disciplines est toujours ce qu'il y a de plus fascinant ».

Vanina Pinter
Ancienne rédactrice en chef adjointe du magazine *étapes:*
et professeur à l'école supérieure d'art du Havre.

written information. For the German studio, all of its projects are considered to be a place for experimentation in which the rule of conduct is to continually stimulate the thought process. In this respect, they recommend working on a variety of projects and finding clients with the desire and courage to make an individual statement. This year they began teaching as guest lecturers at the Offenbach Academy of Art and Design. They are perpetuating this avant-garde precept: "There's nothing more fascinating than the crossing of different disciplines."

Vanina Pinter
Former associate editor of *étapes:* magazine,
lecturer at Le Havre Higher School of Art (ESAH).

CIRCULATION
CLIENT : EMC
DIRECTION ARTISTIQUE : MATTHEW BAGWELL

CIRCULATION
CLIENT: EMC
ART DIRECTION: MATTHEW BAGWELL

13

designergußsæp / 084 / PIXELGARTEN

designerguide / 084 / PIXELGARTEN

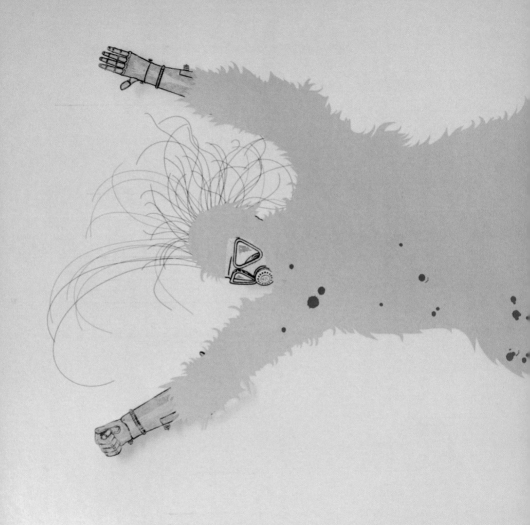

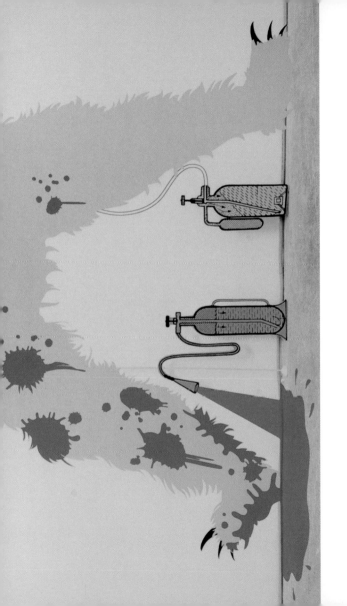

designergußsap / 084 / PIXELGARTEN

ILLUSTRATION, AFFICHE ET COUVERTURE
POUR LE 50E ANNIVERAIRE DU MAGAZINE
SUISSE ALLEMAND *FORM*

ILLUSTRATION, POSTER AND COVER DESIGN
FOR THE 50TH ANNIVERSARY ISSUE OF THE
SWISS GERMAN DESIGN MAGAZINE *FORM*

form

The Making of Design

form 214, Mai/Juni 2007, Deutsch/English, www.form.de

Deutschland 16,50 EUR, Österreich 17,50 EUR,
Belgien 19 EUR, Schweden 180 SEK, Schweiz 32 CHF,
Slowakei 790 SK, Spanien 20,50 EUR

Eff! Oh! Err! Emm!
Celebrating 50 Years of form

PAGE 22 :
EIGENES UND FREMDES IM SCHÜTTELBAD
DIGITALEN DESIGNS
COUVERTURE DU LIVRE PUBLIÉ SOUS LA
DIRECTION DE SEBASTIAN OSCHATZ/MESO

PAGE 22:
EIGENES UND FREMDES IM SCHÜTTELBAD
DIGITALEN DESIGNS COVER DESIGN FOR A
PUBLICATION BY SEBASTIAN OSCHATZ/MESO

PAGE 23 :
COUVERTURE DU LIVRE *THREE D – GRAPHIC*
SPACES DE GERRIT TERSTIEGE (ED.)
CLIENT : BIRKHÄUSER

PAGE 23:
COVER DESIGN FOR THE BOOK *THREE D –*
GRAPHIC SPACES BY GERRIT TERSTIEGE (ED.)
CLIENT: BIRKHÄUSER

PAGE 24-25 :
COUVERTURE DU LIVRE
TACTILE – HIGH TOUCH VISUALS
CLIENT : GESTALTEN

PAGE 24-25:
COVER DESIGN FOR THE BOOK
TACTILE – HIGH TOUCH VISUALS
CLIENT: GESTALTEN

Tactile is a collection of cutting-edge work that illustrates how designers from various disciplines are implementing their ideas in three-dimensional space. The book documents innovative spatial work in creative media from typography and posters to products and installations. Although the examples are often playful, Tactile proves that spatial innovation in graphic design is not limited to personal work or artistic endeavours, but is also a serious trend for commercial applications.

Die Gestalten Verlag
ISBN 978-3-89955-200-3

9 783899 552003

designergußsap / 084 / PIXELGARTEN

UN
FOLDED

PAPER IN DESIGN, ART, ARCHITECTURE AND INDUSTRY

PETRA SCHMIDT AND NICOLA STATTMANN

PAPER GOES 3D

BIRKHÄUSER

UN
FOLDED

PAPIER IN DESIGN, KUNST, ARCHITEKTUR UND INDUSTRIE

PETRA SCHMIDT UND NICOLA STATTMANN

PAPER GOES 3D

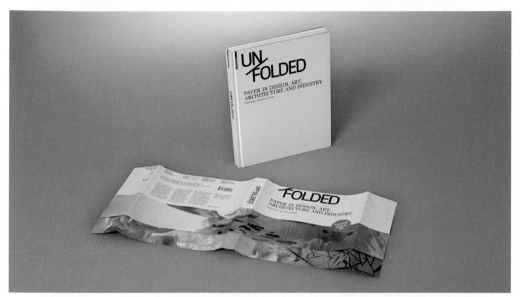

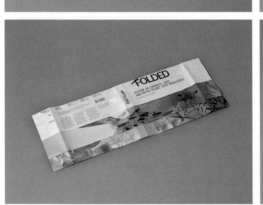
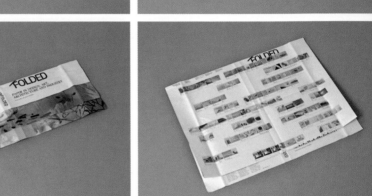

DESIGN DU LIVRE *UNFOLDED – PAPER IN DESIGN, ART, ARCHITECTURE AND INDUSTRY*, SOUS LA DIRECTION DE PETRA SCHMIDT, JOURNALISTE SPÉCIALISÉE DANS LE DESIGN, ET NICOLA STATTMANN, CRÉATRICE DE PRODUIT ET EXPERTE EN MATÉRIAUX. CE LIVRE PRÉSENTE DIVERS PROJETS EN PAPIER ISSUS DES DOMAINES DE L'ART, DE L'ARCHITECTURE, DE LA MODE ET DU DESIGN DE PRODUIT. IL EST DIVISÉ EN DEUX PARTIES : LES PROJETS PUIS LES MATÉRIAUX.
CLIENT : BIRKHAÜSER

DESIGN FOR THE BOOK *UNFOLDED – PAPER IN DESIGN, ART, ARCHITECTURE AND INDUSTRY*, EDITED BY DESIGN JOURNALIST PETRA SCHMIDT AND PRODUCT DESIGNER AND MATERIAL EXPERT NICOLA STATTMANN. THE BOOK SHOWS PROJECTS MADE OUT OF PAPER FROM THE FIELDS OF ART, ARCHITECTURE, FASHION AND PRODUCT DESIGN. IT IS DIVIDED INTO TWO SECTIONS, PROJECTS AND MATERIALS, WHICH SHOWS A VARIETY OF SPECIAL PAPER MATERIALS.
CLIENT: BIRKHAÜSER

EN COLLABORATION AVEC MASAYA ASAI ET TAKAYUKI NIIZAWA DE TBWA\HAKUHODO, NOUS AVONS CRÉÉ LES VISUELS POUR LE GRAND MAGASIN LAFORET DE TOKYO (ÉTÉ 2008), LES AFFICHES ONT ÉTÉ CRÉÉES À PARTIR DE DEUX DÉCORS COMPOSÉS DE CADRES EN BOIS SUR LESQUELS ÉTAIENT FIXÉS DES ÉLÉMENTS TIRÉS DE BANDES DESSINÉES. LES POSTERS SONT AINSI DES PHOTOGRAPHIES D'UNE INSTALLATION EN 3D. CHAQUE CADRE EN BOIS MESURAIT 1,80 M DE HAUTEUR.

CLIENT : LAFORET HARAJUKU
AGENCE : TBWA\HAKUHODO
DIRECTEUR DE CRÉATION : MASAYA ASAI, TAKAYUKI NIIZAWA
DIRECTEUR ARTISTIQUE / DESIGNER : MASAYA ASAI
PHOTOGRAPHE : TAKAKAZU AOYAMA

IN COOPERATION WITH MASAYA ASAI AND TAKAYUKI NIIZAWA FROM TBWA\HAKUHODO, WE CREATED THE VISUALS FOR THE LAFORET GRAND BAZAR SUMMER 2008 FOR LAFORET DEPARTMENT STORE IN TOKYO. WE BUILT TWO SETS OF POSTERS WITH COMICS-INSPIRED WORD BUBBLES THAT WERE THEN PLACED IN WOODEN FRAMES. EVERYTHING THAT WERE THEN PLACED IN WOODEN FRAMES. EVERYTHING THAT CAN BE SEEN ON THE POSTERS WAS BUILD AS A REAL 3-D OBJECT. THE HEIGHT OF EACH WOODEN FRAME WAS 1.8 METERS.

CLIENT: LAFORET HARAJUKU
AGENCY: TBWA\HAKUHODO
CREATIVE DIRECTOR: MASAYA ASAI, TAKAYUKI NIIZAWA
ART DIRECTOR/DESIGNER: MASAYA ASAI
PHOTOGRAPHER: TAKAKAZU AOYAMA

SUPER MARIO FASHION
SET DESIGN FOR THE SUPER MARIO FASHION
STORY IN THE NOVEMBER ISSUE OF *NEON*
MAGAZINE
CLIENT: NEON MAGAZINE

PHOTOGRAPHY: MARKUS BURKE & RODERICK
AICHINGER
PRODUCTION/ART DIRECTION: JONAS NATTERER
STYLING: MAIKE ROHLFING

SUPER MARIO FASHION
DÉCOR DU SUPER MARIO FASHION STORY
POUR LE NUMÉRO DE NOVEMBRE DU
MAGAZINE *NEON*
CLIENT : NEON MAGAZINE

PHOTOGRAPHIE : MARKUS BURKE &
RODERICK AICHINGER
PRODUCTION / DIRECTION ARTISTIQUE :
JONAS NATTERER
STYLISME : MAIKE ROHLFING

MEAN BOOKS
CLIENT : NEON MAGAZINE

MEAN BOOKS
CLIENT: NEON MAGAZINE

THE A TO Z OF MOSQUITOS
CLIENT : NEON MAGAZINE

THE A TO Z OF MOSQUITOS
CLIENT: NEON MAGAZINE

designerguß|sap / 084 / PIXELGARTEN

PAGE 36 À 39 :
PICTURE PUZZLE
CLIENT : NEON MAGAZINE

PAGE 36 TO 39:
PICTURE PUZZLE
CLIENT: NEON MAGAZINE

designergußsap / 084 / PIXELGARTEN

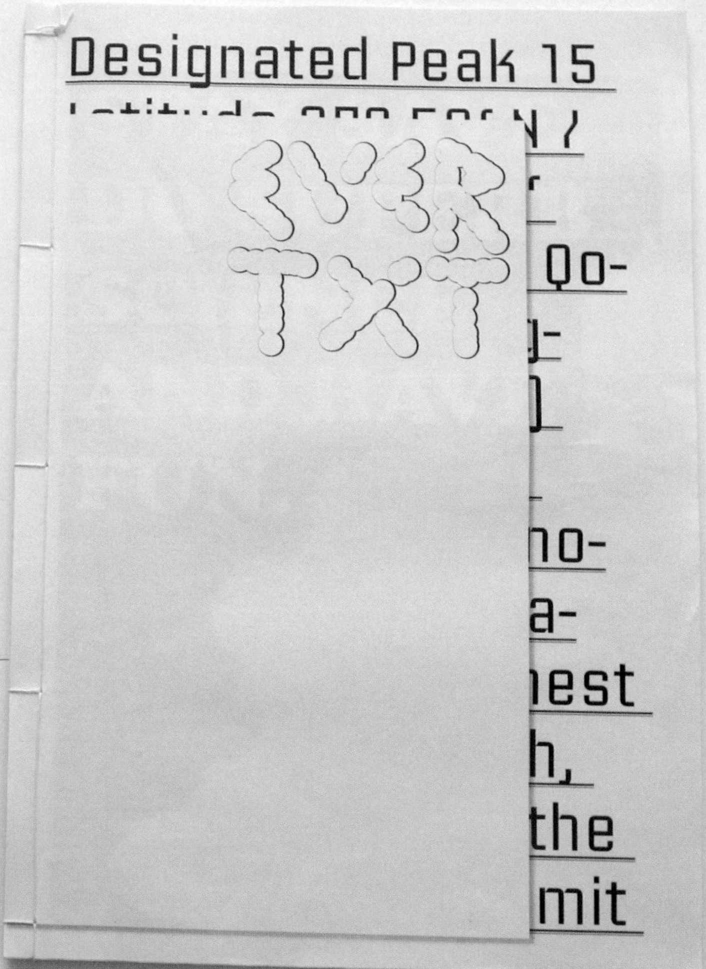

Designated Peak 15

Latitude

EVER
TXT

Qo-

ho-
a-
nest
h,
the
mit

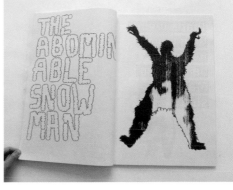

EVER TXT MAGAZINE
MAGAZINE AUTO-PRODUIT PRÉSENTANT
DES HISTOIRES ET COMPTES RENDUS
D'EXPÉDITIONS SUR LA MONTAGNE
LA PLUS ÉLEVÉE DU MONDE

EVER TXT MAGAZINE
MAGAZINE OF READER-SUBMITTED STORIES
AND EXHIBITION REPORTS ABOUT THE WORLD'S
HIGHEST MOUNTAIN

ON MAY 21st 2007
TIM MEDVETZ BECA-
ME THE FIRST FORMER
HELLS ANGELS MEMBER
TO SUMMIT EVEREST /
THE FIRST PLAYMATE TO
SUMMIT EVEREST WAS
POLISH PLAYMATE AND
TELEVISION JOURNA-
LIST MARTYNA WOJ-
CIECHOWSKA ON MAY
28th 2006 / WORLD
RECORD OF EXTREME

IRONING IN HIGH ALTI-
TUDE WAS MADE
BY JOHN ROBERTS AND
BEN GIBBONS WHILE
IRONING IN BASE
CAMP 1 AT 5440 ME-
TERS / LAKPA THARKE
SHERPA IS THE FIRST
MAN TO STAND COM-
PLETELY NAKED ON THE
SUMMIT OF EVEREST
FOR 3 MINUTES /
NUMBER OF DEAD BO-

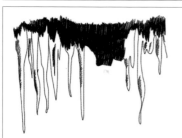

STEP ON THE NITRO

MountainZone.com columnist and sponsored athlete Dave Hahn has just returned from climbing Mount Everest for the fifth consecutive year. This season, Hahn was guiding a party of female climbers on an attempt via the South Col Route. The incident described below took place on the team's final trip down through the Khumbu Icefall, between Camp I and Base Camp.

Khumbu Icefall – I believed that the reality of climbing big mountains was not being shown in American movie theaters. But again, this was all before that morning close to the end of our recent Everest Expedition. I now know that those portrayals are entirely truthful. That fateful morning we started down through the Icefall for the last time, headed for Base Camp and a happy end to our non-Hollywood expedition. We were early in the day; it was still relatively cool and the bridges and ladders would still be nicely frozen. We were moving well after a month and a half on the mountain. Everybody knew which ropes to clip and which ones to avoid. Everybody knew to look at the anchors before trusting them. Everybody knew to watch out for each other and keep moving.

STAY SAVE, DO SUPERB SCIENCE AND HAVE FUN.

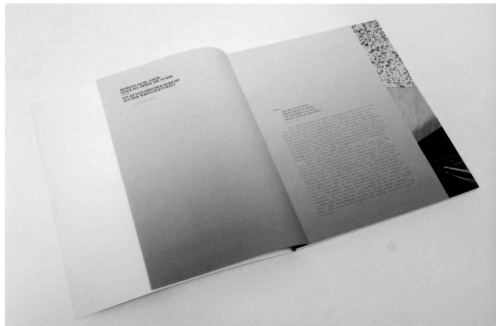

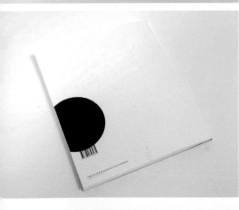

SURFACES
CATALOGUE POUR L'ARTISTE ALLEMANDE
CHRISTINE SCHIEWE
CLIENT : DYNAMO EINTRACHT GRANT

SURFACES
CATALOGUE FOR THE GERMAN ARTIST
CHRISTINE SCHIEWE
CLIENT: DYNAMO EINTRACHT GRANT

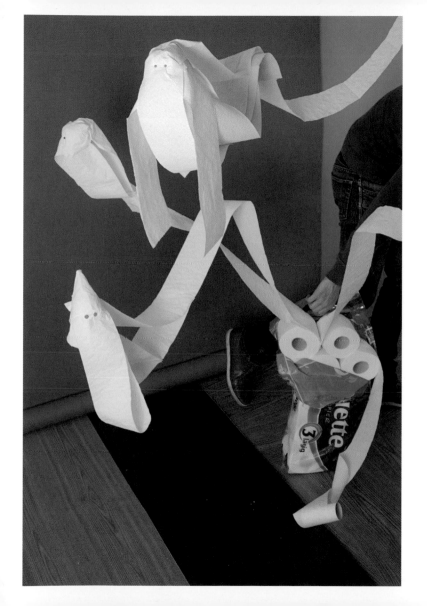

DARUM IST DAS SO
(THAT'S WHY IT IS LIKE THAT)
CLIENT : NEON MAGAZINE

DARUM IST DAS SO
(THAT'S WHY IT IS LIKE THAT)
CLIENT: NEON MAGAZINE

designerɐuɐ̃sap / 084 / PIXELGARTEN

OBJETS
NATURE MORTE À PARTIR DES PRODUITS
DU MOIS DU MAGAZINE *NEON*
CLIENT : NEON MAGAZINE

PRODUCTS
MONTHLY PRODUCTS STILL-LIFE
FOR *NEON* MAGAZINE
CLIENT: NEON MAGAZINE

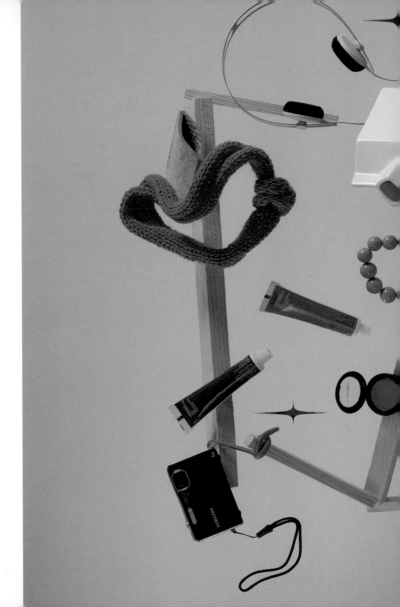

OBJETS
NATURE MORTE À PARTIR DES PRODUITS
DU MOIS DU MAGAZINE *NEON*
CLIENT : NEON MAGAZINE
DE GAUCHE À DROITE :
SEPTEMBRE 2010
FÉVRIER 2011
JANVIER 2011
NOVEMBRE 2010

PRODUCTS
MONTHLY PRODUCTS STILL-LIFE
FOR *NEON* MAGAZINE
CLIENT: NEON MAGAZINE
FROM LEFT TO RIGHT:
SEPTEMBER 2010
FEBRUARY 2011
JANUARY 2011
NOVEMBER 2010

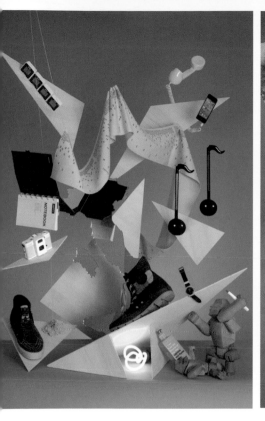

CREATIVE
ILLUSTRATION POUR LA COUVERTURE
DU MAGAZINE *FRM*
CLIENT : FRM MAGAZINE

CREATIVE
COVER ILLUSTRATION FOR *FRM* MAGAZINE
CLIENT: FRM MAGAZINE

ILLUSTRATION D'UN ARTICLE PORTANT SUR LE PHÉNOMÈNE D'OBJETS DE PETITE TAILLE DEVENANT DE PLUS EN PLUS BRUYANTS (COMME LES TÉLÉPHONES PORTABLES) ET DES GROS ENGINS DEVENANT DE PLUS EN PLUS SILENCIEUX (COMME LES VOITURES).

ILLUSTRATION FOR AN ARTICLE ABOUT SMALL THINGS (LIKE MOBILE PHONES) GETTING VERY LOUD AND BIG PRODUCTS (LIKE CARS) TURNING VERY QUIET.

APPS
APPLICATIONS POUVANT ÊTRE UTILES
EN VOITURE
CLIENT : BMW MAGAZINE

APPS
APPS THAT ARE USEFUL IN A CAR
CLIENT: BMW MAGAZINE

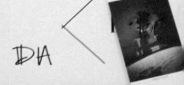

DAADADA
AFFICHE D'EXPOSITION ET CATALOGUE

**DAADADA EST UNE EXPOSITION DES
BOURSIERS DU FAMEUX DAAD, L'OFFICE
ALLEMAND D'ÉCHANGES UNIVERSITAIRES
ELLE PRÉSENTE LES TRAVAUX ARTISTIQUES
DES JEUNES DIPLÔMÉS MAIS AUSSI DES
ÉTUDIANTS DU ROYAL COLLEGE OF ART,**

DE L'UNIVERSITÉ GOLDSMITHS, DE LA SLADE
SCHOOL OF FINE ART, DE LA CENTRAL ST.
MARTINS, DE L'UNIVERSITÉ BARTLETT ET
DE L'UNIVERSITÉ WESTMINSTER.
CLIENT : DAAD, LONDRES

DAADADA
EXHIBITION POSTER AND CATALOGUE

DAADADA IS AN EXHIBITION OF THE
SCHOLARSHIP HOLDERS OF THE RENOWNED
GERMAN ACADEMIC EXCHANGE PROGRAM
DAAD. IT COMBINES ARTWORK FROM RECENT
GRADUATES OR MA STUDENTS FROM THE
ROYAL COLLEGE OF ART, GOLDSMITHS, SLADE

SCHOOL OF FINE ART, CENTRAL ST. MARTINS,
THE BARTLETT AND THE UNIVERSITY OF
WESTMINSTER.
CLIENT: DAAD, LONDON

DAADADA / AN EXHIBITION OF THE
DAAD SCHOLARSHIP HOLDERS 2008/09
EXHIBITION CATALOGUE

01-10-2009
UNTIL
04-10-2009

ADA
STREET
GALLERY
LONDON

INTRODUCTION

CONTEMPORARY GERMAN ART IN
LONDON IS BLEAK THESE DAYS. WHEN
CONTEMPORARY ANYTHING BUT SCARCE.
THE ART BURLINGTON INTRODUCED THE FIRST
UNLIKE LEGENDARY EXHIBITIONS IN THE
GERMAN BURLINGTON INTRODUCED COLLECTIVE
NEW NOT PUBLIC ONLY TO THE »TWENTIETH CENTURY«
1938 NOT PUBLIC FOR LONDON TO
BRITISH AVANTGARDE PROVED THEIR
GERMAN ALSO PROVED FOR THEIR GERMAN
TIME BUT HAVEN EXHIBITS OF GERMAN
BE A SAFE WORKS, EXHIBITION
BANNED NOWADAYS, POPULATE
ARTISTS. NOWADAYS

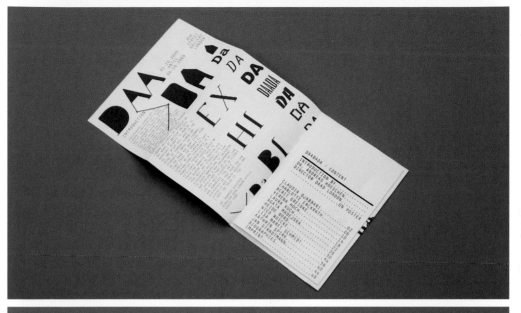

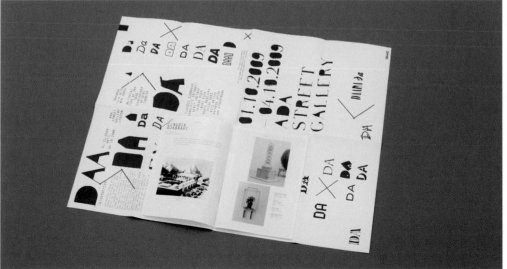

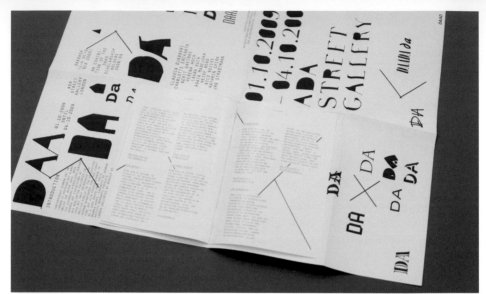

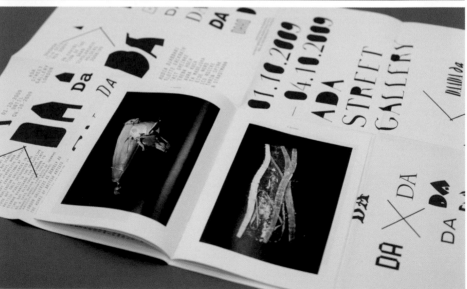

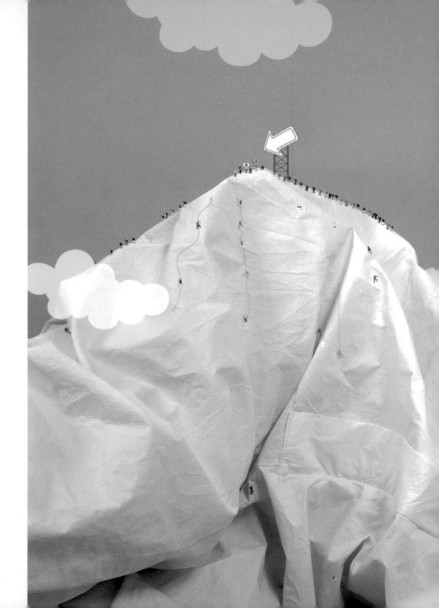

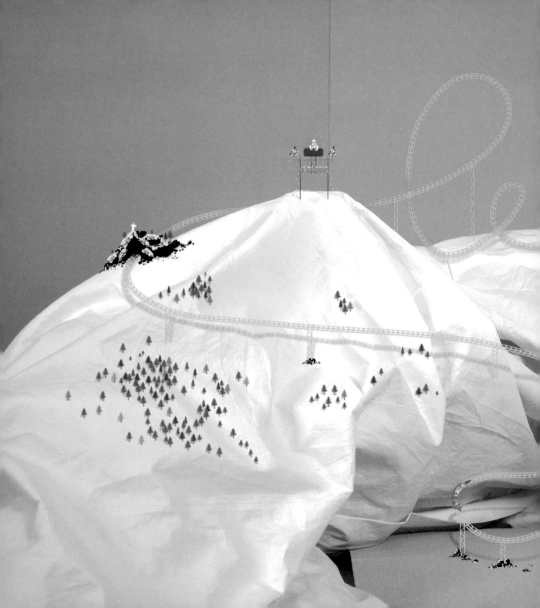

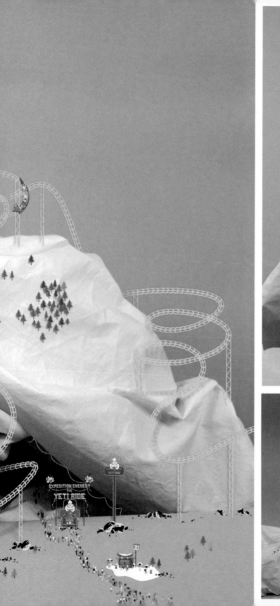

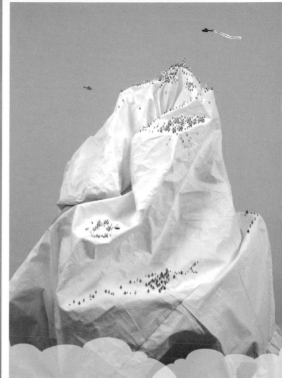

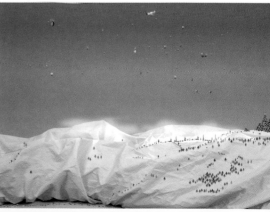

SUSHI MAGAZINE
ILLUSTRATION ET CONCEPTION
RÉALISÉES AVEC CATRIN SONNABEND
ET ANNETTE PFISTERER
CLIENT : ART DIRECTORS CLUB, ALLEMAGNE

SUSHI MAGAZINE
ILLUSTRATION AND DESIGN TOGETHER WITH
CATRIN SONNABEND AND ANNETTE PFISTERER
CLIENT: ART DIRECTORS CLUB, GERMANY

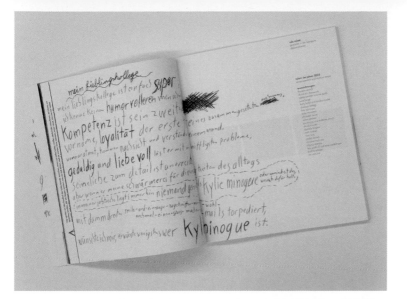

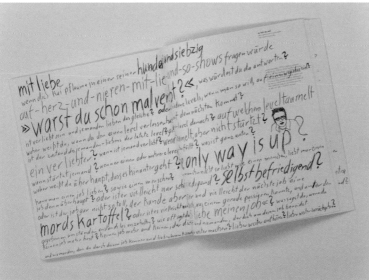

UM WAS ES NICHT GEHT
ILLUSTRATION, PHOTOGRAPHIE,
INSTALLATION

UM WAS ES NICHT GEHT
ILLUSTRATION, PHOTOGRAPHY, INSTALLATION

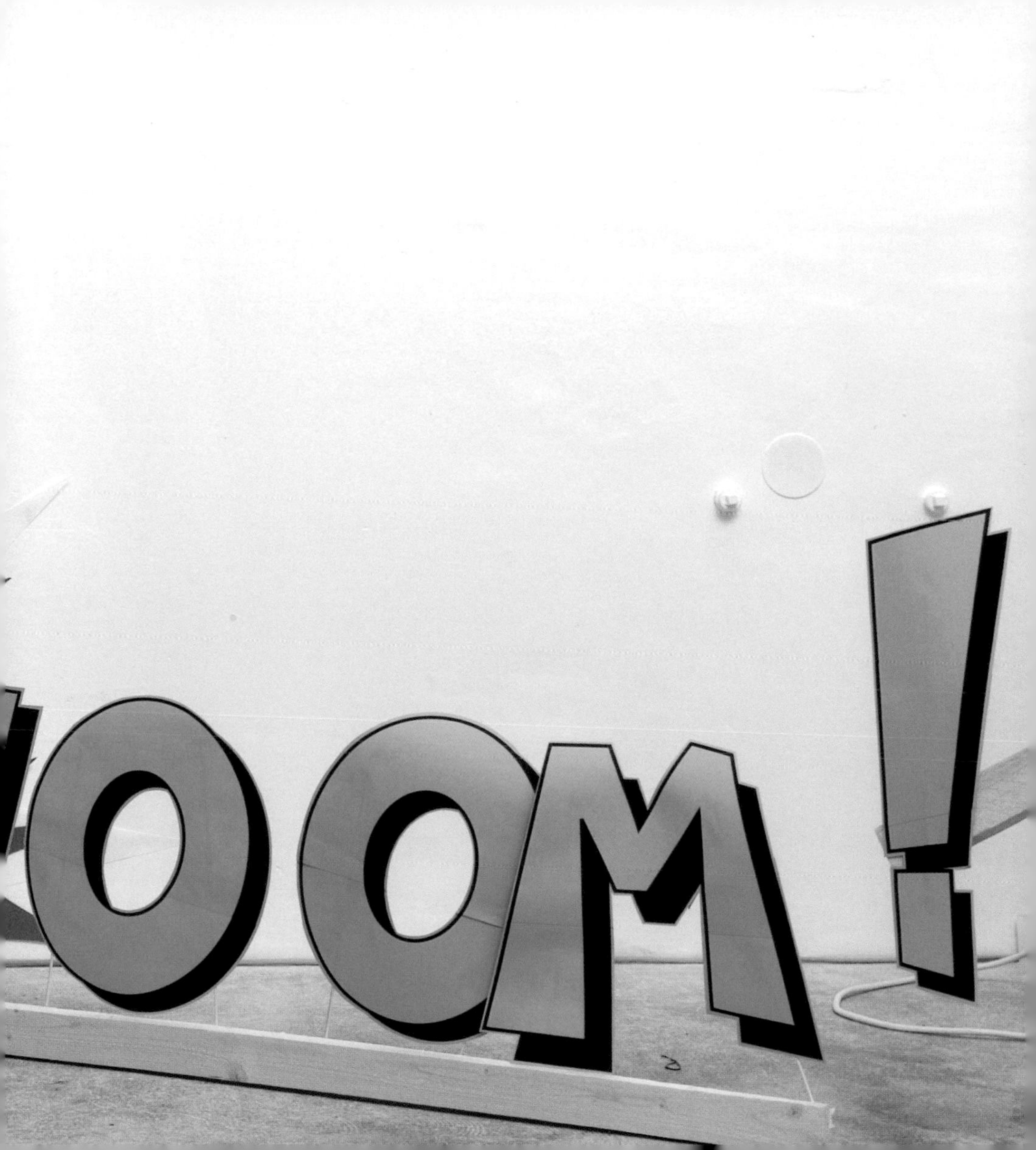
OOM!

UM WAS ES NICHT GEHT
ILLUSTRATION, PHOTOGRAPHIE,
INSTALLATION

UM WAS ES NICHT GEHT
ILLUSTRATION, PHOTOGRAPHY, INSTALLATION

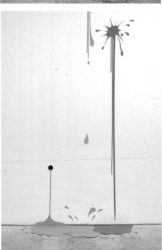

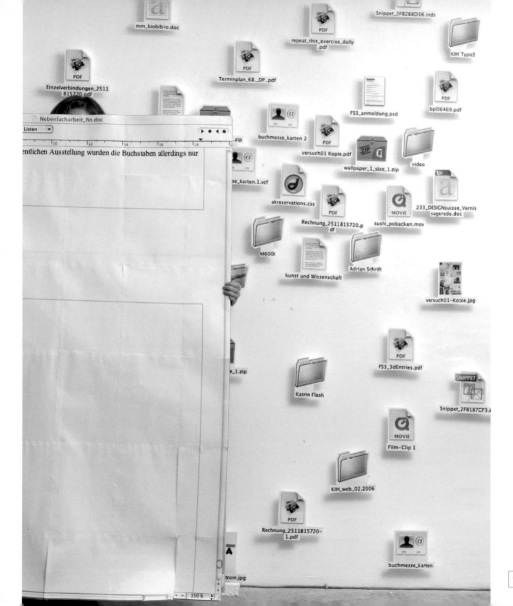

UM WAS ES NICHT GEHT
**ILLUSTRATION, PHOTOGRAPHIE,
INSTALLATION**

UM WAS ES NICHT GEHT
ILLUSTRATION, PHOTOGRAPHY,
INSTALLATION

VERSUCHSANORDNUNGEN DES ERZÄHLENS
DESIGN EDITORIAL, ILLUSTRATION,
TYPOGRAPHIE

VERSUCHSANORDNUNGEN DES ERZÄHLENS
BOOK DESIGN, ILLUSTRATION, TYPE

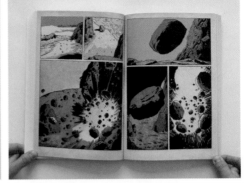

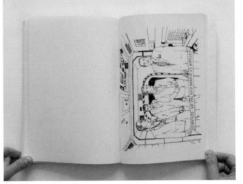

A LOOK BACK AT 2008
NATURE MORTE
CLIENT : NEON MAGAZINE

A LOOK BACK AT 2008
STILL-LIFE
CLIENT: NEON MAGAZINE

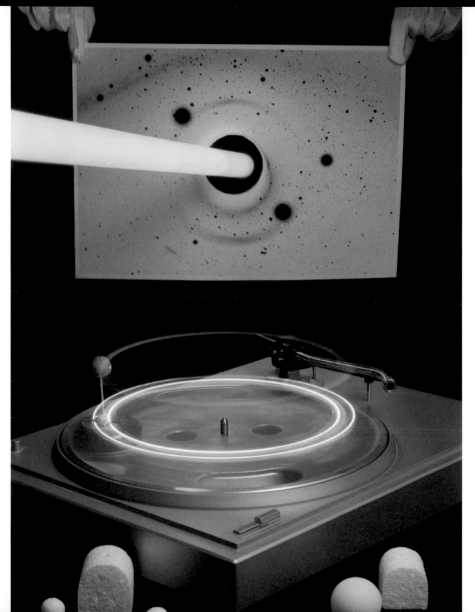

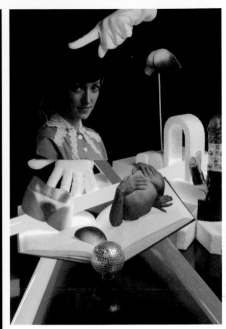

PAGE 90-91 :
PAPER SCOUT
CLIENT : SUSHI MAGAZINE

PAGE 90-91 :
PAPER SCOUT
CLIENT: SUSHI MAGAZINE

EIN HAUFEN MODE
HISTOIRES DE MODE PCUR LE MAGAZINE
INTRO
CLIENT : INTRO
PRODUCTION : AMÉLIE SCHNEIDER

EIN HAUFEN MODE
FASHION STORY FOR *INTRO* MAGAZINE
CLIENT: INTRO
PRODUCTION: AMÉLIE SCHNEIDER

designergußjsap / 084 / PIXELGARTEN

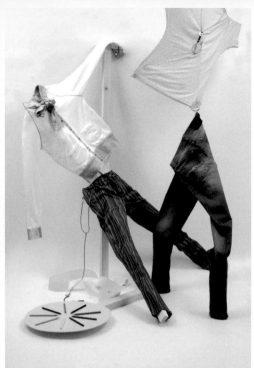

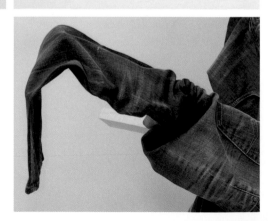

EIN HAUFEN MODE
HISTOIRES DE MODE POUR
LE MAGAZINE *INTRO*
CLIENT : INTRO
PRODUCTION : AMÉLIE SCHNEIDER

EIN HAUFEN MODE
FASHION STORY FOR *INTRO* MAGAZINE
CLIENT: INTRO
PRODUCTION: AMÉLIE SCHNEIDER

TYPICAL GIRLS
POUR LE PROJET DE LIVRE
INTITULÉ *TYPOLYRICS*
THE SLITS

TYPICAL GIRLS
FOR *TYPOLYRICS* BOOK PROJECT
THE SLITS

FRANKFURT! FRANKFURT?
DESIGN EDITORIAL POUR UN LIVRE
SUR FRANCFORT
CLIENT : SOCIETÄTS VERLAG

FRANKFURT! FRANKFURT?
DESIGN FOR A BOOK ABOUT
FRANKFURT AM MAIN
CLIENT : SOCIETÄTS VERLAG

FRA
NKFU
RT
!

FRANKFURT
?

EIN PORTRÄT DER STADT,
DER RHEIN-MAIN-REGION SOWIE
ALL DER ANDEREN, GANZ UND GAR
BEMERKENSWERTEN STÄDTE
WIE ASCHAFFENBURG, BAD HOMBURG,
DARMSTADT, HANAU, MAINZ,
OFFENBACH, RÜSSELSHEIM & WIESBADEN,
DIE IN DER UMGEBUNG DER
EINZIGEN DEUTSCHEN
METROPOLE LIEGEN – GEZEICHNET
IN GENAU
44
HÖCHST
ABWECHSLUNGSREICHEN KAPITELN.

ALL DAS HERAUSGEGEBEN VON
DR. CHRISTIAN ANKOWITSCH

SOCIETÄTS**VERLAG**

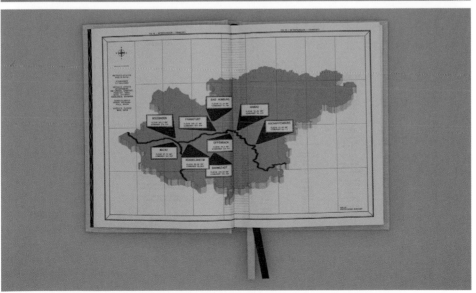

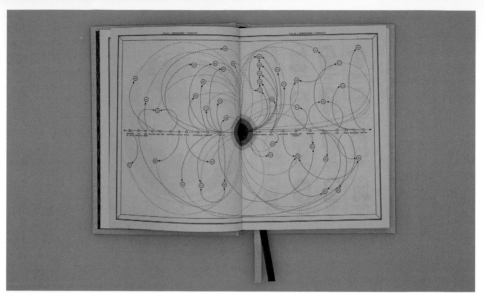

I WENT THERE ONCE.

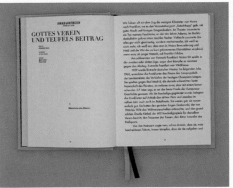

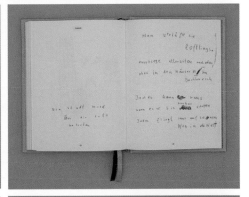
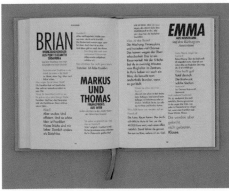

VISA WIRE HEADS
PROJET POUR LE DESIGN D'UNE NOUVELLE
CARTE DE CRÉDIT PERSONNALISÉE
IMPRESSION ET FORME AUX NORMES
DE L'ANTENNE RFID
CLIENT : VISA EUROPE

VISA WIRE HEADS
CONCEPT FOR A NEW PERSONALIZED CREDIT
CARD DESIGN
PRINTED AND SHAPED RFID ANTENNA
CLIENT: VISA EUROPE

09.2008
Thomas Gärtner
7463 8574 7382 6372

09.2008
Inga Rydbeck
7463 8574 7382 6372

09.2008
Thomas Diekmann
7463 8574 7382 6372

09.2008
Elvis Huber
7463 8574 7382 6372

09.2008
Agathe von Lilienfeld
7463 8574 7382 6372

09.2008
Günther Koslowski
7463 8574 7382 6372

09.2008
Uta Maria Hilmer
7463 8574 7382 6372

09.2008
Mike Jeckelson
7463 8574 7382 6372

09.2008
Mandy Wiesner
7463 8574 7382 6372

09.2008
Stefanie Petermann
7463 8574 7382 6372

09.2008
Jan Phillipp Golder
7463 8574 7382 6372

09.2008
Susanne Beimershagen
7463 8574 7382 6372

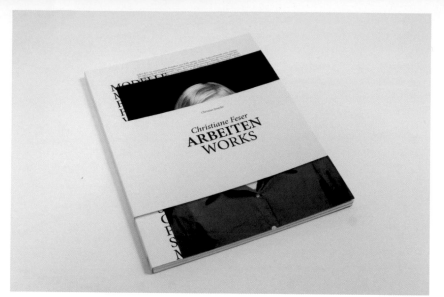

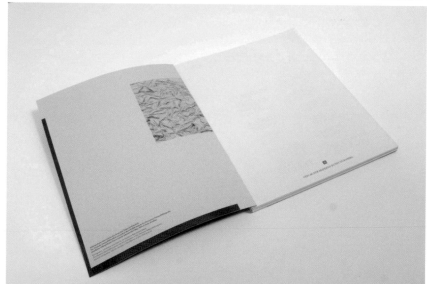

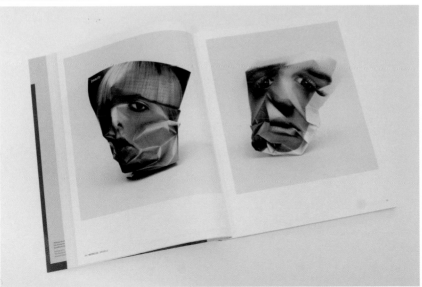

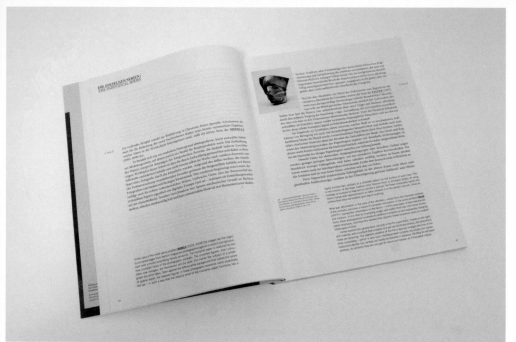

FALTEN /
FOLDS

WIESE AM REITHLIFT / MEADOWS NEXT TO REITHLIFT

2007 / Monitor, Holzstele, Trackball / monitor, wooden stele, trackball

Hochauflösendes Bild, konstruiert aus etwa 400 digitalen Fotografien, gezeigt auf einem Wandmonitor. Mittels Trackball wählen Betrachter Ausschnitte und zoomen bei konstanter Bildschärfe durch Szenerien, die anfangs mit bloßem Auge nicht erkennbar waren. / High-res image, constructed from about 400 digital photos, shown on a wall monitor. Viewer can select sections by trackball and zoom through scenes initially not evident to the naked eye – with no loss of focus.

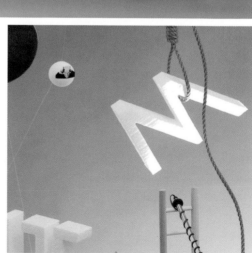

MUT
ILLUSTRATION POUR LE MAGAZINE
ALLEMAND *BEEF*
CLIENT : BEEF MAGAZINE

MUT
ILLUSTRATION FOR THE GERMAN
MAGAZINE *BEEF*
CLIENT: BEEF MAGAZINE

PAGE 116-117 :
6M1P
ILLUSTRATION POUR LE MAGAZINE
FRANÇAIS *6M1P*
CLIENT : 6M1P

PAGE 116-117:
6M1P
ILLUSTRATION FOR THE FRENCH
MAGAZINE *6M1P*
CLIENT: 6M1P

ÜBER MUT

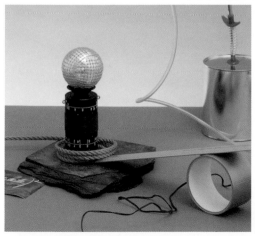

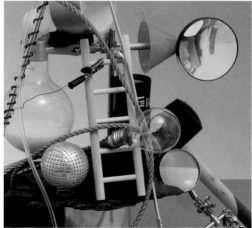

DEMONSTRATING PRODUCTS
ILLUSTRATION POUR LE MAGAZINE
KULTURSPIEGEL
CLIENT : KULTURSPIEGEL

DEMONSTRATING PRODUCTS
ILLUSTRATION FOR *KULTURSPIEGEL*
MAGAZINE
CLIENT: KULTURSPIEGEL

REMERCIEMENTS / ACKNOWLEDGMENTS:

Thanks to our families, our friends and all the people who have helped us and worked together with us: Catrin Sonnabend, Alexander Lis, Sebastian Pataki, Kai Bergmann, Johannes Fuchs, Luzia Kälin, Mareike Gast, Nicola Stattmann, Jörg Gimmler, Bianca Stich, Lucia Cinefra, Christopher Tauber, Marcus Gundling, Christian Ankowitsch, Tanja Pfoser, Svetlana Jakel, Valerie Christoph, Kai Linke, Hardy Burmeier, David Heßler, Tobias Lindner, Christiane Feser, Karin Aue, Verònica Aguilera, Petra Schmidt, Gerrit Terstiege, Karianne Fogelberg, Sophia Muckle, Heiner Blum, Klaus Hesse, Eike König, Jonas Natterer, Markus Burke, Roderick Aichinger, Jakob Feigl, Amelie Schneider, Andreas Liedtke, Ulrike Grünewald, Peter Müller, Kilian Schindler, Oli Vainamo, Masaya Asai, Taketo Oguchi and all other friends we might not have mentioned here, all the supporters, clients and collaborators over the years.

Céline Remechido, Vanina Pinter, Émilie Lamy and the Pyramyd team for their patience with us and their hard work to make this book possible.